SRA
OPEN COURT READING

Fred

A Division of The McGraw·Hill Companies

Columbus, Ohio

www.sra4kids.com

SRA/McGraw-Hill

A Division of The **McGraw·Hill** *Companies*

Printed in the United States of America.

Send all inquiries to:
SRA/McGraw-Hill
8787 Orion Place
Columbus, OH 43240-4027

ISBN 0-07-569455-7
   3 4 5 6 7 8 9 DBH 05 04 03 02

"Ham, Sam Clam?" called Fred.
"Not ham," clicked Sam Clam.

"Grab a top hat, Bill Bat," said Fred.
"No top hats!" snapped Bill Bat.

"Jump in the jug, Ben Bug," said Fred.
"It's snug as a rug."
"No jug," grumped Ben Bug.

"Melted fudge, Judge Jed?" called Fred.
"Not melted fudge," huffed Judge Jed.

"Fig, Pat Pig?" called Fred.
"Not figs!" puffed Pat Pig.

"Who wants my stuff?" Fred sniffed.